I0488548

Mentoring Startups Entrepreneurs

Part II

Dhananjaya Parkhe
1st Edition

Recently the Sad story of my favorite Terris Star Boris Becker was published in media. One story doing rounds on WhatsApp groups was:

Quote"Boris Becker had it all — six grand-slam tennis titles, models hanging off his arm and luxury houses all over the world.

At the height of his career, the German ace had amassed a reported $63 million in prize money and sponsorships, but now the man once known as "Boom Boom" for his ferocious serve has gone from boom boom to bust.

Now 49, Becker was declared bankrupt by a British court Wednesday, capping a fall-from-grace story that saw the one-time wild child go from Wimbledon champ to walking headline by blowing through money, women and business ventures in retirement.

His lawyer pleaded for more time and "one more chance" to make good on debts he has racked up in retirement. But the judge said, regretfully, the man she had once watched dominating center court has already had plenty of chances. "One has the impression of a man with his head in the sand," Registrar Christine Derrett said. : End Quote

This followed some morals and learnings (Teachings):

The above news of Boris Becker, six times grand slam winner and one of the most successful tennis player, becoming bankrupt sends one of the most powerful message to all the wengsters of today.

 "Success is never permanent . Plan well when the sun is shining coz failing to plan is planning to fail. "

*Financial management is most crucial lesson one should learn in these uncertain times. *

Getting Started

In this Part of our Mentoring eBook we shall talk about the Successes and failures of Enterprises, Startups and established businesses. As a Mentor, I like to share the experiences without judging and I am usually "Non-prescriprive" as I believe that I am a Mentor who has walked this path before like any walker and while I can navigate, I am not a Doctor to prescribe a medicine. That is the job of Doctors - The Consultants in business. Here I am restricting myself to being a Mentor and I leave judgements to the adult reader who KNOWS what is Right and Wrong and has a Conscience to discern the Truth and false. I remember my Mentor once saying to me "Don't ever try and change and Adult - We can't! And then he would jokingly ask - has our wife been successful changing we?

Chapter Number 1
Whether U Hire Slow OR Hire Fast. Just Fire Faster
Human Resource Management

New Mantras for the Start Ups/ Entrepreneurs as HR Strategies I read recently.

1. Hire Slow, Fire Fast. 2. Hire Fast, Fire Faster.

Both are meant to satisfy the Investors; both are being said to be Sure-Shot formula of success. I wonder !

Let me explain why? To my mind the auto recall (No I don't mean the Toyotas Auto Recall) is "Theory is One Man's Opinion !" is what I read somewhere and " The more times you repeat the Lie, people are likely to believe it as gospel truth" AND the printed word is usually to be taken as Cast in Stone". Thus, spoke - Goebbels ? : P (I read recently that Internet is famous for the most Misquoted Quotes :). So, pardon my ignorance about who said what, I doubt that these statements about Hiring or Firing have been subject to any serious scrutiny and scientific analysis. The written word prevailed and continues as gospel Truth. (Unfortunately, that is :) .

I worked over the years for several corporations including Start Ups, Private and Public Sector Companies, Owner driven company and MNCs. I also had an unsuccessful stint as Entrepreneur once.

One of the Key learning as a Profit Centre Head for me was: " The toughest decision here is to Add a Head Count and to get a Capex Approved". No. It wasn't about bureaucracy management (:)) or perhaps it was ! Those were also the most challenging years and most successful ones for me! They were also the Best for Top Line, Bottom

Line growth. We had the best of Customer Satisfaction Index, Best of Employee Satisfaction Index and many Excellence parameters. For our discussion, today - Let's forget the Capex: D and focus instead on Hiring and the two Start Up success formulas listed above. (After all, this is a 6-12% cost discussion, compared to Capex which may hit the Balance sheet over 3-5 years positively or otherwise).

Let's now see the Practical side of it and how does the Entrepreneur/ HR recruiter looks at it when they decide to Hire Slow and Fire Fast ! I saw this good article on Forbes.com

I found three issues here:

1. "I don't typically hire someone who has been with a competitor because I've found that those employees tend to be set in their ways and tougher to train. I hire people that can be trained and cultivated into my company's culture."

Personally, I differ. If you take the decision to Hire Slow - it does not mean that you would compromise the 'Scale up Fast' and 'Grow Top Line quickly' Objective. So, I would look for a competitor hand who can make following three possible.

a. Bring customers who are dissatisfied with competition and willing to move their business lock, stock and barrel and do not mind doing business with a Start Up.

b. Bring customers who are willing to share the Increase in their annual demand for goods or services which the Start Up offers to the marketplace.

c. Has enough Database of his own to not make Cold Calls (and I firmly believe that Cold calling is dead - and yes, it is a theory - a single man's opinion.

By doing this, the only additional resource I use is in Right Equipping of the individual hired and do not incur any Onboarding, On the job training costs which any Start Up would find hard to fund.

2. "Finding someone you like and your team likes can take a long time. Don't rush it.

When you do find someone that works, be sure to set up training and mentoring programs for that new employee".

I differ with this too. The business stage of Start Up does not allow an entrepreneur this liberty. Yes, with hiring experience this can be a factor one can check which is primarily about social abilities, attitude of the new Hire. For customer facing staff of the Start Up - Training Yes - mentoring NO is my belief for the stage of the business.

3. These programs ensure the employee follows your procedures and processes and help to build and reinforce your corporate culture.

To my mind, a Start Up venture is an evolving business. if it already has copious Procedures and Processes written out - it is carrying of old bricks to build a new business or simple copy and paste job. In my view, this is likely to be a success barrier as it is unlikely to create a sustainable edifice - a New business organization without bias.

Hire Fast and Fire Fast - i shall discuss the Hire Fast part here. Fire Fast being common element in both

Proponents of this theory believe "I'll know the right employee when I see him/her".

Really? And, you're also certain that once you hire that job candidate he/she will meekly give in when you decide to Fire Fast ? The prospective employee will not have a long, successful career objective as one of your employees.

5 questions will help HR Managers hire right...and faster

1. Who exactly do we wish to hire? Clarity is critical—and this means across the entire organization from the recruiters to the interviewers, including the hiring officials. I have seen the Fast Ramping Up organizations focus on the Quantity First and Quality is last on their mind.

2. How will we evaluate candidates? What is usually absent is Documented, well-defined, specific criteria are best when evaluating candidates.

3. How would we keep the qualified candidates engaged? The idea here is to Screen and Sell the job in a Start Up to the qualified candidate.

4. How Do we eliminate quickly? The Screening and evaluation process needs to be simple and Fast. In the interview process, evaluate your non-discretionary criteria upfront so you have visibility to this and can immediately filter out these candidates. I call it failing fast!

5. How Do we finish well? How do you extend the job offer. Is this well prepared and carefully considered. If you want to pass on the candidate - what is the line of communication.

Let us now deal with the Common Strategy prescribed " FIRE FAST !"

Some simple Recipe's for Firing Fast: :)

1. Don't Pay wages on time.

2. Create cumbersome procedures for Claims, Commissions, Bonuses and Incentives.

3. Micro Manage - especially the Field and customer facing staff.

4. Execute Office Politics well.

5. Use an Abrasive and Arrogant style of communication.

My Suggestion:

A. Fire Fast strategy - Charity begins at home. Begin from the Top. Heard this comment before ? "I had asshole CEOs. When we hit a bump in the road he was very quick to slash-and-burn."

B Never regret firing anybody. Not once.

C. If you wish to regret, regret not firing somebody quickly enough.

D. Don't take any pride in letting somebody go. YOU may be the Next ! :)

E. If the sacking is legitimate, chances are they know in their gut it isn't working and will appreciate the candor.

F. You recognize Fire Fast decision can impact somebody three ways :

I. Economically. ii. Personal Life. iii. It is a big blow to the ego. If you are afraid of Firing - you cease to be an entrepreneur - You are a Philanthropic. No startup company has any spare capacity for dead weight.

Fire Fast - thus is not promotion of slash-and-burn employee culture.

Fire Fast is not about creation of a constant revolving door. I

Fire Fast is also not against meritocracy and demotivating the best staff from rising to the top.

Fire Fast would mean that Age and experience are not relevant.

Good people get ahead, bad people would get asked to leave, as would bad performers !

The Fact is - Many Companies Hire Fast but Fire Slow OR Hire Slow and Fire Slow at Start Up stage.

It pays to Check your legal framework. It helps to Get your papers in order. It helps when we Treat people with respect and professionalism. Being open and productive; honest with them about their shortcomings or why they aren't working culturally.

But fire them quickly. Don't tolerate Non-Performance, Integrity issues or Bad Attitude.

There ! I Said it !! :)

Disability is No Barrier

The story went viral on WhatsApp and I was very happy to share it with others.

Hats Off to Srikanth Bolla ! 24-year-old blind (Visually Challenged for the sophisticated) entrepreneur from Hyderabad.

When he was born, his parents, who were earning Rs 20,000 in a year, were advised to get rid of him, but somehow he survived.

Despite getting 90% in class 10th, he was not allowed to choose Science stream for 12th; he sued the State Govt., fought for 6 months, and won the case. He scored 98% with Science in 12th.

When IITs and NITs didn't give him hall ticket for writing competitive exams, he applied overseas, and got selected in 4 of the best colleges ever created on the Globe: MIT, Stanford, Berkeley, and Carnegie Mellon.

He chose Massachusetts Institute of Technology, received a scholarship, and was MIT's first International blind student.

After returning from US in 2012, he launched Bollant Industries, where 60% of employees are poor, physically challenged. This 450 employees company is now worth Rs 50 crore, and recently, Ratan Tata invested in his venture.

As per him, "I was made blind by the perception of people.." When the world said to him that you can't do anything, Bolla said, "But I look up at the world and say I can do anything."

Salute Respect   .

Disability and being physically challenged is no barrier for DIVYANG JAN as the PM of India calls them.

Their grit, determination and courage are worthy of praise. Not only they generate Profits - they generate employment for others with their passion as a Side Effect.

Chapter Number 3

Wearing Calipers - Startup
Journey of Divyang Entrepreneur

I am Sharing a real-life experience of a startup from Part II of my next eBook "He wasn't called 'Physically challenged' or the fancy Indian name given by an Indian Politician as "Divyang" in current times; he was affected by Polio in childhood and one leg was weaker and thinner than the Right Leg and people called him Lame in front of him to constantly remind of his disability.

I met him when I was 12. I had lost my father and had shifted town to be with closer family for support. He was our neighbor - elder to me by 6 years, was struggling with his Science Graduation exams year on year. His parents were considered outcast by close family - Mother a Sindhi and Father a Gujarati businessman. The only brother was a Doctor and Captain in the Army.

We became friends soon. Mr. T and another of his friend Mr. G both had similar vibes. Same college failures, similar habits, failed love affair and similar hobbies - travelling, biking, sightseeing. Mr. T's father had a Surgical instrument company for which he would obtain yearly orders from School and college labs and Government hospitals. Business was not very good - they were Mid-Rich family.

Mr. T with his disability had worked out on his Arms and they were very strong and could shame a Good wrestler/ boxer. He was a good bike driver and with his powerful arms would kick the toughest of bikes with his hands. He also drove at breakneck speed and driving with 'No hands 'on the handle was his specialty. Some of these traits were rubbing off on youngsters like me who did workout on our Arms with dumbbells and weightlifting and learning to drive bikes as if we were getting to do a Tattoo exhibition in a Police parade ground.

Mr. T's mom was a stickler for discipline and was a Principal of a Girls High school. He constant taunts troubled Mr. T and he began spending time in fathers' shop sometimes visiting hospitals, colleges to get orders. He had moderate success in this.

His fertile brain was quicker 'Mechanical' though. He bought a .5 HP bike and removed every single part. Learnt to re-assemble the bike with the help of a friend. Then moved on to a Vespa Scooter and did the same. He then drove from Raipur to New Delhi alone to meet his brother who was posted there. This was inspiring. The .5HP Vicky bike broke down several times but he had learnt to handle all situations so carried on.

He then bought a Scrapped Morris 8 Car which the owner had stripped to the last part as the parts were not available for replacement in the local market. The Doctor owner did not have time and energy to repair it. Mr. T bought it cheap for INR 600. He then went to Mumbai by train, searched the parts bought them and booked them in the break van of the train all by himself. With the help of a friendly mechanic, they assembled the car in a few months on the road (no workshop) and took it for a ride. The thought in his mind was to open a foreign car repair workshop and parts showroom. He took this car with spoked wheels to many nearby towns with friends. Overall a dynamic and hardworking personality.

A couple of years later, he went to Mumbai and realized that Fish was brought from Mumbai as well as Calcutta by train to Raipur in break Vans. He had a breakthrough idea. He decided to bring colored / decorative real fish and create Aquariums for Home Decor.

The idea was unique. He tested with his Rich/ Semi Rich friends, Hotels, Clubs and with colleges. He had the lukewarm response but one single order. He got Glass, found a glass cutter, an iron fabricator and a putty-like thing (No M-Seal or Aluminum Angles or Double Glazed glass in those days). Visited Mumbai and carried live decorative fish by train. 50% of them died. He then put them in the Glass aquarium created and sold it. He also kept one in his surgical goods showroom which drew the huge crowd of children, students and adults alike. People like the different colored fish and wanted to know how expensive the hobby is. Awareness levels in this small town of about 500,000 people were extremely high and people knew who supplies fish aquarium made of glass and iron for home decor and get them fish and fish food from Mumbai.

Making the Glass aquarium was tough. He would do the assembly with his own hands while we friend would watch him toil. He would not delegate buying and transporting fish/fish food work to anyone. Later he also brought a bubble maker so that oxygen would flow into the water. He also began bringing variety into the fish by bringing shark-like fish, tortoise, snake-like fish etc. as Novelty to meet the demand of the customers who demanded them.

Business was good. When I remember this nearly 50-year-old real story - it is a story of a physically challenged person who was determined had grit, courage and terrific will power to not just show initiative but FINISHIATIVE in what he decided to do.

When I look at the today's Startups they are no different. They are budding entrepreneurs with one or two ideas which they wish to pursue at all costs. Mr. T had friends like us, a very supportive father and a huge network. He had a gift of gab but generally, he was a straight talker who would not mince words but nobody who knew him took him otherwise.

A Disabled, differently abled, Divvying could do this 50 years ago and I believe that even today with the right support they can do well rather than being dependent. My friend had to visit Mumbai every year to change his Calipers which supported his left - weak leg and as he had to stay for a month in Mumbai for this - he began getting ideas. Shall share some of these in my Mentor talks/ lessons in coming days.

When I reflect, it is with nostalgic memories I remember my friend who despite his few vices was very dear to all of us in the family. "

Chapter Number 4
Why does your Startup need a Mentor?
Mentoring Startups

As an entrepreneur, I have learnt that life is tough and unpredictable. I was faced with many doubt and challenges. Nary a times, I found myself lurching from one problem to another.

Having a Mentor or two at hand in those troubled times may have changed my life completely. I honestly believe so !

I strongly believe that mentoring should be voluntary and Free. While you may charge people for Coaching/ Executive Coaching - it is my firm belief and I do mentoring totally Free. It gives me a choice - the choice to say NO 1 MENTORING is a thus a valuable business resource for any company, especially for startup stage companies. In past 3-4 years, I was invited and joined many website - both Private Mentoring Platforms and Business Associations Mentoring Platforms and the fact is I did not get a single email thereafter either from the people inviting or from any Startup Entrepreneur ! And people say that in India finding a good mentor is difficult. In fact, I'd say that entrepreneurs in India can access better funding with ease if they can find good mentors!

A good mentor adds enormous value business enterprise. As the Startup scene in India hots up the need for REAL, GOOD Mentors will be felt and will be a scarce resource ! IAs an entrepreneur, you may be wondering: 'how exactly will a mentor add value to my company?'

How is this possible?

As a Mentor, I am not afraid to hold a mirror to your business:

As a mentor, I objectively assess the state of your business and the direction in which it is headed. I help bring in an unbiased point of view. In doing so, I act as a mirror, reflecting the state of your business exactly as it is: with warts, moles, blemishes and all. I identify what's right and what's wrong with your business (or the business plan, depending on when exactly the mentor is brought on board) and help you fix things that need to be fixed.

Each Mentor has a different Style I have two unique styles.

1. To gain Trust I reveal myself - transparently with my Failures and Follies first at times calling myself a Failed Entrepreneur. I allow them to be critical and share their views as to what could have happened if I had a Mentor or what I could have done differently.

2. Second style is from my coaching lessons. I tell the protégé'/ mentee that I shall CHALLENGE/ PROVOKE them the point when sometimes they would feel like they made a mistake taking me on board as Mentor . In 99% cases, it works and the Mentees benefit as this helps. The Anger is channelized into creative/ positive energy and looking at possibilities and newer ways of doing things.

If there is something wrong with the business (such as a weak process, poor accounting standards, and a bad marketing plan, whatever) I point it out to them and nudge you to take corrective action. I had launched a software based Business Plan, Marketing Plan course in a business school way back in 2000. It was a software developed and we bought from Prof. Tim Berry and his firm.

I ask tough questions:

From time to time, the mentor acts as an examiner who poses tough questions to you, the entrepreneur. Not to needle and rattle you, but to get you thinking about improving things in your company. If the mentor does not perform this role diligently, complacency will most likely set in, giving you and you team the feeling that all is well, when all may not be well.

A mentor's questions could pertain to the business model itself, the definition of target customers, the customer acquisition cost, the delivery times and SLAs, the time taken for the business to break-even, the extent of capital investment needed, the systems and processes being adopted, …. anything. For instance, I have seen mentors advise entrepreneurs to temporarily apply brakes on their efforts to develop the 'perfect' product and instead, go get their first set of paying customers.

I sometimes will make you step back:

For a Mentee who was getting African students job ready who were studying in India but were not employable in their own country after studies I suggested a Paradigm shift. The unfortunate students were being beaten up and were under attack in different towns. I suggested the Mentee to look at the possibility of signing MOUs in African countries and shift base of business completely. I also suggested 1. to have a Train the Trainers program in Africa for the students who complete his course and 2. Create a steady stream of rotating Trainers who would visit African offices to teach the course for 3-6 months and return after completion of the course.

Because you have your nose to the grind always — operationally speaking — the mentor will pull you back a step every now and then, and make you see the big picture. He helps you to look at the changes that are happening around you, which may have a bearing on your business. For instance, changes in consumer mindset, distribution channels, technology, law, etc. could all affect business and so, must be constantly factored into your planning.

He will open doors for you and making his connections work for you.

As a prolific Networker for over 15 years, I open my network for my Mentees. As an entrepreneur, one of the biggest roadblocks you will face is a lack of professional contacts such as domain experts, service providers and potential employees. Sometimes the biggest issue is finding normal support systems like stationery, photocopying, Scanning, Lamination, binding and other office supports. For instance, your business may need a website designer, an auditor, a part-time Chartered Accountant, someone who will help you register the company, help you with Memorandum of articles and association, keeping minutes, guiding you with legal and compliances, keeping tax records, and other contacts in prospective client companies and an event manager, not to mention an investor. The mentor can make a few calls and put you in touch with the relevant agencies and people. It is up to you to take it from there.

Mentor will push the bar higher:

Entrepreneurs are often an unsure lot. While they want to make it big, deep down they are not sure if they will manage to achieve BIG goals. They are not sure how much to push themselves. A good mentor will demolish this self-doubt, instill large doses of confidence in the entrepreneur and make him push the bar high. As the saying goes, it is only when you aim for the stars that you will reach at least the moon.

Mentor will share his value system with you:

A good value system and work ethic are most important to a fledgling organization. If set up early, they can take the organization a long way. They help maintain a clean and healthy working environment. A mentor will share his professional value system with you and to the extent relevant, and get you to incorporate it in your organization.

Mentor will motivate you and make you laugh:

All the grind must be balanced with large doses of humor. A mentor with a sense of humor can indeed be a great asset to your business. His joie de vivre is likely to rub off on you and your team, with the result that all of you unwind occasionally and keep celebrating successes along the way. You will even learn to laugh hysterically at your mistakes and move on. All this eases the working atmosphere tremendously and helps you retain your sanity.

The mentor will also pat you on the back occasionally for a job well done or for a milestone achieved, thereby egging you on further.

Mentor will teach your patience:

The quest for success and for greatness is often long. You must weather many a storm and keep digging deeper into your reserves of strength, creativity and resilience. A mentor's sagacity will prove invaluable at such times. He will urge you not to fret (which is anyway useless), but to keep chipping away patiently.

The mentor has a big role to play in calibrating your tempo, curbing your impatience and helping you keep the faith.

In sum, a good mentor keeps his cross-hairs firmly on the interests of the business and from time to time, gives you the necessary inputs. And so, if you haven't brought a mentor or two on board your company yet, do it right away!

(In referring to mentors, I have used the masculine gender merely for ease of writing and not because of a gender bias!) and I have met in my lifetime able and efficient lady mentors personally who were as good and at times much better !

A Short Guide to the Life Stages of a Startup is shared below:
The distinct phases that mark the roadmap of a startup from selection of an idea to converting it into reality. I describe what you need to be prepared with at each stage and offer you tips collected from real mentors, investors and accelerators. Preparing for Your Entrepreneurial Journey.
Those who Aspire to become entrepreneurs must be well-prepared in

life as a startup. The first few years are invariably hard, even if your business venture is doing much better than you planned.

1. Concept Stage and Idea Selection

Often entrepreneurs have many ideas or concepts that they are equally excited about. And all of those could become very good business opportunities. However, it is important for entrepreneurs to choose ONE idea that they will pursue.

2. Idea Validation

Every entrepreneur is super-excited with their idea. While you need to be passionate about your idea it is also critical to understand if there is a large enough market for that idea, and whether your intended users are as excited about the product/service as you are.

3.Starting up

A startup is not about an idea or a concept. It is about building a real business around that idea or concept.

4. Early Stage

The initial days are the toughest. Your concept, business model, pricing, and other strategies are likely to be tested in the market. And often challenged.

3. Early-Growth Stage

Once you have found the 'product-market fit', the business will get into an early-growth phase and then start growing. This is where most ventures fail as entrepreneurs may not have built a foundation that will help them scale their venture. or concept.

Chapter Number 6

Success is going from failure to failure
Never Give Up

My biggest learnings are from the Business Failures. Failures are things we wish to hide from others. A Good Mentor never hides them from his Mentees and uses them for Trust Building and learning thru his own life case studies. Failures are not something to feel ashamed or vulnerable or apologetic.

Like Hope we should be on good terms with Failures. There is nothing negative about it. At the core of every Successful person it is seen that at the core there is failure. If we learn our lessons from failures well, we can then lead and mentor others to be successful.

How to Reset our Mindset and negative thinking about failures?

It would need new understanding of what failure means. We need to grasp that it doesn't mean game over simply means to try, try again, next time with more experience. And if this is accepted as true, failure will be opportunity for us to begin again intelligently. To do so, though, we need to learn the reasons why failures happen ?

Here are a few of the most common reasons of Failures:

1. A fixed and lumpy thinking and negative mindset. It's satisfying to believe that what you know and how you know it is always the right way, but of course we don't know it all. Instead we need a growth mindset, one that believes there's always something to learn, something to grow with, something to get better at. it doesn't

matter how slowly you go if you don't stop.

2. Stagnant development. Most of us can get far on our natural strength, gifts and talents. But at some point, we may discover we don't have the skills we need to keep advancing, and we find ourselves at a standstill. To grow, we need to always keep developing ourselves. If we stop learning, we stop growing.

3. No clear purpose. if you aren't sure where you're going, it's natural to get lost, repeatedly. To briefly wander off the path is one thing, but to not have a goal, a purpose, doesn't allow you to plan. And, as the old saying goes, when you fail to plan you are planning to fail. Your purpose is the place where your deep determination meets the impact you want to make.

4. Negative thinking. Few things are more destructive. Nothing ever good has ever come from negative thinking; instead, it feed our shame and vulnerabilities. If you want to succeed, learn the power of positivity and what it can do when you are trying to achieve something difficult. Think of failure as unfinished success.

5. Lack of productivity. This makes perfect sense. Without action, there is no productivity; without productivity, there's no achievement; without achievement, there's no success. Your future is created by what you do today, not by what you do tomorrow. Nothing will work unless you do. Even a little progress each day can yield big results.

6. Lack of motivation. If you don't want to fail, you must start working toward success. If it's important to you, you'll find it within you to get it done. If not, you'll find excuses--and then failure is just around the corner.

7. Shortage of confidence. Without confidence, where you are going to get the strength to move forward? Confidence is especially needed when failure presents itself. Your confidence is the most important factor in your achievement.

Failure will present itself to all of us sooner or later. But knowing how to respond, is up to us.

Non-Compliance to Laws and Rules - Sure Failure!
What a Startup Needs to comply with?

A Startup can come into trouble by Non-Compliance. There is no such thing as "First Break all Rules" in business. A Startup moving towards becoming an Entrepreneur and finally a full-fledged Businessman/woman must take pains to know what one MUST do.

(This list is compiled from Government, industry association and other sources and to acknowledge all of them in this short space is not possible but my gratitude and thanks to CII where I am a registered Startup Mentor and other friends in the media for their support in compilation)/

Let us Start with Incorporation

For the sake of simplicity, this Chapter divides Indian startups into two broad categories –

Startups planning to engage in manufacturing activities and

Startups who are planning to engage in providing services (including software/technology-driven products and services).

Applicable Compliances for these two categories are further sub-divided into

Statutory Compliances and

Non- Statutory compliances

We are not discussing the Social Entrepreneurship Startups - the NGOs, Trusts, Societies, Welfare Associations here.

Statutory compliances are ones which emanate out of a specific enactment or rules framed thereunder—for example, the requirement to obtain registration certificates for opening shops or offices, arising out of the Shops and Establishments Acts of different states.

Non-statutory compliances are not directly related to any specific legislation, but arise because of adhering to such legislations. But more on that later.

Once we have clarity on the business model/idea, the very first requirement should be that of choosing the type of corporate entity under which we want to establish our venture.

We have the options to choose from – a company, typically a private limited company (governed by Companies Act) and a limited liability partnership (governed by the Limited Liability Partnership Act).

Most startups choose the Pvt. Ltd., since private limited companies by their inherent legal nature, provide better security for both promoters as well as investors who are funding the venture.

Once we have decided upon establishing a private limited company as our vehicle of choice, we must have it registered with and incorporated at the Registrar of Companies (Rock). That entails that we along with our co-founders/co-promoters subscribe to a Memorandum of Association (Moan) and drafting Articles of Association (Aloe).

We will also need to provide several documents and fill all the appropriate forms and affidavits. An important compliance to be noted here is that while registering the name of the company, the words "Private Limited" must be present.

Choose unique name for the company

Since we are on the topic of names, let's look at our first non-statutory compliance. We want to register a company name. It must be unique, yet relatable. How else are we going to create a niche space in the market for our self? So, our first task is to do a name search with the Rock to check whether someone else has already registered the name, which we wish to put on record for our company. This is a non-statutory compliance – in that, it arises because of we adhering to the statute (in this case, the Companies Act).

Setting Up and Running our Manufacturing Unit

So, we're done with incorporating the company; we're now in business. Welcome to the world of compliances. If we're in the manufacturing sector, our first instinct will be to set up a manufacturing unit – a factory. We'll have to buy land for the factory. During and post purchase of that land, we need to apply for clearances and NOCs (No Objection Certificates) from the local and municipal authorities under the Panchayat Raj Act or the Municipal

Act of the state where we wish to set up our operating unit

Now that we own the land and have our clearances, we will want to start construction of our factory. We will be faced with compliances under the Factories Act. Depending on the state in which our factory is located, we will need to apply with the Chief Inspector of Factories and Boilers for a 'stability certificate'. This document certifies that the design of our factory is safe for workers and the surrounding areas and that production can begin once construction per this design is completed. The Factories Act is both an enabling as well as welfare legislation. It facilitates construction of factories and ensures health and safety of workers.

For example, if we plan on building a factory in Maharashtra, we'll require :

NOCs from the local Gram Panchayat (under the Panchayat Raj Act) or Municipality (under the Municipal Act) Consent to Establish (CTE) and/or Consent to Operate (CTO) under the Water (Prevention and Control of Pollution) Act and the Air (Prevention and Control of Pollution) Act, from the State Pollution Control Board (SPCB). The SPCB permissions are critical to the operation of the factory, since funding is often tied to the viability of the project. The SPCB permissions ensure smooth development of the factory and thus facilitate the inflow of funds secured through loans or equity. A trade license (Certificate of Enlistment) from our local Panchayat/Municipality, which allows we to run a business/trade in our choice. Once our factory is up and running we will be required to adhere to numerous compliances under the Factories Act – related to operations, and health and safety of our workers.

Office Space

We will also need office space – for a sales office, or a registered office. We might wish to open branch offices in other cities/towns – now we will be required to obtain registration under the Shops and Establishments Act of the State where our operating units are based. We will start recruiting employees for which we will now face additional compliances under labor laws such as Payment of Wages Act, Minimum Wages Act, Payment of Bonus Act, Employees State Insurance Act (if our employees earn below a certain threshold), Contract Labor (Regulation and Abolition) Act (in case we employ a certain number of contract laborers. These labor law compliances are often applicable across both the manufacturing as well as the services sectors.

Compliances in the IT/Its Sector

The Information Technology Act provides an overarching policy framework; along with its attendant Rules, the Act gives rise to several critical compliances. For example, the Sensitive Personal Data or Information Rules under the Act mandate that – all sensitive personal data that is collected from clients/customers may only be gathered after clear, written consent has been obtained. The Rules also state that companies, which gather such data, must publish a clearly drafted privacy policy on their websites – a fundamental compliance, which many companies have not even heard of. The Act and attendant Rules mandate that we obtain ISO/IS/IEC 27001 or equivalent certification, especially while providing cloud services.

Compliance requirements vary not just by the nature of our business but also by its scale and size; the geographical location and our corporate structure. This article gives an indicative list of things that a startup needs to consider at the time of setting up by taking two examples – a manufacturing company in Maharashtra and an IT/Its company in Karnataka. These are given in the next part of this article.

Corporate Compliances (Common to Maharashtra and Karnataka)

Obtain digital signatures – Obtain digital signature from authorized DSC issuing authority (as listed in the MCA 21 portal) for at least one director to sign E-forms.

Obtain Director Identification Number (DIN) – Every individual to be appointed as a Director of our Company must apply to the Ministry of Corporate Affairs (MCA) for DIN in Form DIR 3.

Name availability of proposed company – Application for reservation/availability of name of the company must be made to the MCA in Form INC 1. (Note: Name will be valid only for a period of 60 days from date on which application for reservation is made)

Preparation of memorandum of association (Moan) and Articles of Association (Aloe) – Draft MoA and AoA for our company. The main objects of the MoA and the AoA must match the objects written down in Form INC 1.

Application for incorporation of a private company – Apply to RoC, within whose jurisdiction our registered office is located. Application must be made in Form INC 7 along with Form INC 22 and Form DIR 12. Requisite documents must be appended to these forms.

Requirement for Company Secretary (CS) – In case the paid up share capital of our company exceeds Rs. 5 crore, we are mandated to appoint a whole-time Company Secretary.

Labor Compliances

Manufacturing (Maharashtra)

Payment of Gratuity Act, 1972

Submit notice of opening of factory in Form A to controlling authority.

Employees' Provident Fund Act, 1957

Register our establishment with the EPFO.

File monthly PF returns with the EPFO.

Employees' State Insurance Act, 1948

Obtain registration of our factory by applying in Form 01.

Contract Labor (Regulation and Abolition) Act, 1970

Register as a principal employer by filing an application in Form I (upon employing 20 or more contract laborers).

Industrial Disputes Act, 1947

Form one or more Grievance Redressal Committee (upon employing more than 20 workmen).

Form a Works Committee (upon employing more than 100 workmen).

Motor Transport Workers Act, 1961

Obtain registration for our establishment (if we employ more than 5 motor transport workers (includes drivers, cleaner, transport cash clerk, watchman or attendant) at least 30 days prior to start of operations, by applying in Form I.

Child Labor (Prohibition and Regulation) Act, 1986

Display a notice in Marathi and English specifically mentioning the prohibition of employment of child labor in our factory.

Labor compliances

IT/ITeS (Karnataka)

Payment of Gratuity Act, 1972

Submit notice of opening of factory in Form A to controlling authority.

Employees' Provident Fund Act, 1957

Register our establishment with the EPFO.

File monthly PF returns with the EPFO.

Employees' State Insurance Act, 1948

Obtain registration of our factory by applying in Form 01.

Contract Labor (Regulation and Abolition) Act, 1970

Register as a principal employer by filing an application in Form I (upon employing 20 or more contract laborers).

Industrial Disputes Act, 1947

Form one or more Grievance Redressal Committee (upon employing more than 20 workmen).

Form a Works Committee (upon employing more than 100 workmen).

Motor Transport Workers Act, 1961

Obtain registration for our establishment (if we employ more than 5 motor transport workers) at least 30 days prior to start of operations, by applying in Form I.

Child Labor (Prohibition and Regulation) Act, 1986

Display a notice in Kannada and English specifically mentioning the prohibition of employment of child labor in our factory.

Karnataka Shops and Commercial Establishments Act, 1961

Apply for Registration of the Establishment within 30 days from commencement of our establishment in Form A.

Apply to Labor Commissioner in Form R if we intend to employ women employees during night shift.

In case we employ women employees during night, we must comply with best practices to ensure security of women employees as enumerated by the Govt. of Karnataka.

Environment Health and Safety Compliances Manufacturing (Maharashtra)

Environmental Impact Notification, 2006

Obtain prior clearance from Central Govt., before construction of our factory by applying in Form 1.

Air (Prevention and Control of Pollution) Act, 1981

Obtain consent to establish and operate from Maharashtra Pollution Control Board (PCB) by applying in Common Application Form.

Water (Prevention and Control of Pollution) Act, 1974

Obtain consent to establish and operate from Maharashtra Pollution Control Board (PCB) by applying in Form XIII/Form OG.

Bio-Medical Waste (Management and Handling) Rules, 1998

Obtain authorization from Maharashtra PCB for generating bio-medical wastes (from our first aid unit) by applying in Form I.

Environment (Protection) Act,1986 (from DG Set perspective)

Keep the emission and noise level of the generators within prescribed limits after installing DG sets.

Hazardous Wastes (Management, Handling and Transboundary Movement) Rules, 2008

Obtain authorization from Maharashtra PCB for disposal of hazardous wastes by applying in Form 1.

Public Liability Insurance Act, 1991

Obtain insurance policy against liability to provide compensation before handling any hazardous substances.

Maharashtra Fire Prevention and Life Safety Measures Act, 2006

Install fire prevention and life safety measures and get a compliance certificate in Form A from Licensing Agency.

IT/ITeS – Karnataka

Environment (Protection) Act, 1986 (from DG Set perspective)

Keep the emission and noise level of the generators within prescribed limits after installing DG sets.

E-Waste (Management and Handling) Rules, 2011

Obtain authorization from the Karnataka State Pollution Control Board prior to handling and generating e-waste.

Operations Module

Manufacturing (Maharashtra)

Factories Act, 1948

Obtain certificate of stability from a competent person in respect of every work of engineering construction for our factory in Maharashtra.

Obtain prior written approval from the Chief Inspector of Factories for site and construction/extension of our factory in Maharashtra under the Factories Act, 1948 (apply in Form 1).

Obtain registration and license for our factory in Maharashtra under the Factories Act, 1948 (apply in Form 2).

Obtain prior written approval from the Local Authority to connect our factory drainage system to the public courage system.

Obtain prior written approval from the Maharashtra Pollution Control Board (PCB) with respect to arrangements made for disposal of trade-waste and effluents.

Indian Boilers Act, 1923

File an application to the appropriate Inspecting Authority for the registration of boiler in the State of Maharashtra.

Engage an Inspecting Authority for carrying out inspection at the stage of erection of boiler.

Petroleum Act, 1934

Obtain approval for all the following containers having below mentioned capacities from the Chief controller:

i. Containers > 1 ltr (for class A petroleum);

ii. Containers > 5 ltrs (for class B petroleum); and

iii. Containers > 5 ltrs (for class C petroleum).

IT/ITeS (Karnataka)

Information Technology Act, 2000 read with Sensitive Personal Data or Information Rules

Draft and implement a privacy policy for handling of or dealing in personal information (PI) including sensitive personal data or information (SDPI); make sure this policy is available on our website.

Fiscal Module

Manufacturing (Maharashtra)

Income Tax Act, 1961

Application for Permanent Account Number (PAN) in Form 49-A.

Application for obtaining Tax deduction and collection account number in Form 49-B.

Chapter V of the Finance Act, 1994

Obtaining service tax registration by applying in Form ST-1.

Maharashtra Value Added Tax Act, 2005

Application for registration in Form 101.

Maharashtra Tax on the Entry of Goods into Local Areas Act, 2002

Application for registration in Form 1.

Central Sales Tax (Bombay) Rules, 1957

Application for registration certificate in Form A.

Central Excise Act, 1944 read with Central Excise Rules, 2002

Register at www.aces.gov.in. Post registration, fill Form A-1 in the "Reg" tab. Print the filled form and submit it. Take a printout of the filled form as well as the acknowledgement of submission. Submit the aforementioned printouts to the relevant Excise authorities with requisite documents.

Authorizing Factory Head (who should be a Director of the Company) through Board Resolution.

IT/ITeS (Karnataka)

Income Tax Act, 1961

Application for Permanent Account Number (PAN) in Form 49-A.

Application for obtaining Tax deduction and collection account number in Form 49-B.

Chapter V of the Finance Act, 1994

Obtaining service tax registration by applying in Form ST-1.

Karnataka Value Added Tax Act, 2003

Application for obtaining VAT registration in Form VAT-1.

Central Sales Tax (Karnataka) Rules, 1957Application for registration certificate in Form A.

Non-Statutory Compliances (applicable to Maharashtra and Karnataka)

It is often found that during day-to-day operations of the company, we require various documents as a matter of necessity. Therefore it is often prudent as well as expedient for we to have well-drafted copies of the documents listed below.

Collaboration Related Agreements

Memorandum of Understanding (MoU)

Franchise Agreement

Profit/Revenue Sharing Agreement

Strategic Alliance Agreement

Confidentiality Related Documents

Non-Disclosure Agreements (NDA)

Confidentiality Agreement

Website Related Documents

Terms of Service Agreement

Privacy Policy (has been mentioned under IT Act, 2000)

Additional Disclaimers

Terms of Use

Shrink Wrap/Boiler-Plate Agreements

Disclaimer: This is not a comprehensive list. For detailed list and explanations thereof and all the requisite policies, procedures, rules - please contact the appropriate competent authority for information.

www.ingramcontent.com/pod-product-compliance
Lightning Source LLC
Chambersburg PA
CBHW081314170526
45166CB00011B/3530